AT HOME IN MAINE

Houses Designed to Fit the Land

Text by Christopher Glass

Photographs by Brian Vanden Brink

Sitting in its small clearing by a pond, this rebuilt Colonial in Standish embodies the best traditions of locating a house in harmony with its natural environment. See Page 47.

Text copyright © 2004 by Christopher Glass
Photographs copyright © 2004 by Brian Vanden Brink

Design by Chilton Creative

Printed in China

5   4   3   2

ISBN number: 0-89272-639-3
Library of Congress Control Number: 2004116484

Down East Books
P.O. Box 679
Camden, ME 04843
A division of Down East Enterprise,
publishers of *Down East* magazine

For catalog information and book orders,
call 800-685-7962, or visit www.downeastbooks.com

DEDICATIONS

To my teacher Vincent Scully, who taught me to look for the builder's intention in any structure. To my guide Craig Eder, who tried to get me to view those intentions with charity. To my wife, Rosalee, who gives me the strength and courage to do what needs to be done.

—C.G.

To my father, who taught me the value of hard work and the pursuit of excellence. To my mother, who taught me that "man does not live on bread alone but on every word that comes from the mouth of the Lord." To my wife, who always encouraged me to pursue my dreams and the work I love, even when we did not know how things would turn out. To my daughter, who is a constant source of joy and pride to her mother and me.

—B.V.B.

CONTENTS

CONTENTS

ACKNOWLEDGMENTS

The idea for this book came from Chris Cornell of Down East Books, and I am in his debt for the opportunity to present my thoughts about house design through this collection. Chris has been supportive throughout the writing process, recognizing the difficulty I have had fitting the work into a schedule of active practice and teaching at Bowdoin College.

Brian Vanden Brink's photographs make this book possible. His technical skill and his eye for the beautiful picture complement the artistry of the designers of the houses shown in these pages.

The writers of the articles that appeared in *Down East* magazine with these photographs have provided me with the background on the houses and have given me good information about the owners and designers. These stories presented the houses as they are used and thought about by their owners, and conveyed the excitement of living in a house that does more than provide shelter.

The owners are the ones responsible for enabling these houses to come into being. Though architects sometimes joke that a client is the architect's means of producing a house, without the determination of the owners to create a beautiful place in the world, the architects would not have had the chance to help them.

The builders of these houses are the unsung heroes of architecture. Magazines often extol the owners and architects, but seldom the craftsmen whose labor produces the actual structure. Maine is blessed with many careful and competent builders who take pride in their craft, and these houses were a chance for them to do their best work.

And finally there are the architects. Architects often don't get along with each other, or with clients and developers and builders, because they disagree on the details of the design and are sometimes fiercely protective of their own ideas. That said, they share a passion for building well. For them, a house is not a commodity to be bought and sold, but a work of art that expresses the joy of living in harmony with the land.
—C.G.

ACKNOWLEDGMENTS

When Kathleen and I moved to Maine in 1978, we didn't know anyone here, had never lived in the state, had never been in business before, and really did not know how we would survive in Maine. We didn't even know that I could earn my living in photography; it was a dream that we were pursuing.

Much has happened since then, and this book represents the efforts and labor of many people, not just me. First of all, I want to thank God for giving me work that I love and find meaningful. To have joy in one's profession is a gift that I do not take for granted. I am privileged to be able to work with beauty in a spectacular environment with the light and shadow that only God can make. I am convinced that much of what people respond to in these photographs is that light.

My clients have designed and built the structures that I have photographed. I am honored to work with such gifted and creative home owners, architects, and craftsmen.

Architectural photography is physically demanding, arduous work. The hours are long, and the travel is burdensome, but I have been blessed over the years with excellent assistants, without whom I could not have produced the photographs in this book. I want to thank Bill Thuss, Chris Gelder, Dan Yovanovich, Kevin Shields, Trevor Davis, Eric Lee, Doug Hayward, and especially Todd Caverly.

The staff of *Down East* magazine gave me the earliest opportunities to have my work published, and I owe them a debt of gratitude. Over the years they have given me assignments that have been both rewarding and fun. The people at the magazine have been wonderful to work with. I offer my heartfelt thanks to Steve Ward, Dave Thomas, Dale Kuhnert, and Dawna Hilton.

I also want to thank Chris Cornell at Down East Books for bringing Chris Glass and me together for this book project. Chris Glass has done an outstanding job of putting these photographs into an understandable, informative, and readable context.

Lynda and Thad Chilton, who designed this book, are to be recognized and thanked for doing a great job and for being flexible and easy to work with.

—B.V.B.

Part One
THE TOUCHSTONES OF GOOD DESIGN

We who have lived and worked in Maine for the last few decades have seen changes in the way people think of house design. Before the middle of the twentieth century, homes were generally either farmhouses or town houses, with a few cottages by the seashore and camps by the lakes. Once the automobile began to make the suburbs accessible, we saw subdivisions begin to surround Maine towns and cities, creating areas that were neither farm nor town nor woods, populated by neither farmhouses or town houses or camps or cottages, but instead by the generic structure we call the suburban house, styled to resemble a Colonial or ranch or even log cabin.

We have seen a steady increase in the areas devoted to the suburbs, and as such tracts have grown, we have all become more and more aware of what we lose when suburbs take over. Town centers decay and are abandoned in favor of car-friendly shopping centers, and open farmland is replaced by stretches of nearly identical houses placed close together on lots just large enough that they feel more open than town lots. The natural landscape is flattened and cleared and generally ignored. Houses are oriented to the street without thought for sun and view, and new materials like vinyl siding make them seem alien to the traditional and natural environment.

But there have always been exceptions to this all-too-

The Gothic cottages of Bayside demonstrate that bigger isn't necessarily better. See page 66 for a new Gothic cottage.

*Opposite — Stonington's village of houses, fish sheds, and an Opera House steps down from the woods to the shore. **Above** — A summer cottage on Little Deer Isle uses a sweeping roofline and weathered shingle siding to keep from dominating its site.*

familiar picture, and it is the aim of this book to draw attention to a variety of them. The houses you will see are widely varied in style and history, but they have in common owners who share a respect for the land and an informed understanding of how to express that respect in the way their houses are designed and built. I will try in my descriptions to highlight the aspects of design that distinguish these dwellings from the typical off-the-shelf

suburban house, so that the care with which they suit their settings and the environment becomes evident.

The houses that follow are by no means the only ones to show these qualities, nor are they necessarily the "best" houses in Maine. The principal selection process was quite simple and, to an extent, quite arbitrary. The houses are chosen from among those that have been photographed by Brian Vanden Brink, one of the nation's

Left — *A Cape in Eastport is at home on its promontory.* **Above** — *The Shaker Village at Sabbathday Lake is a tight cluster of white clapboard buildings set amid pastures and woods.*

most skilled architectural photographers, who makes his home in Maine. All but one have been published by *Down East* magazine. Beyond those two practical criteria, the choices have been mine. Most of the houses that follow are on sites along the coast, though there are a few from up-country. In today's Maine, most of the building activity that produces the kind of thoughtful house design I am interested in presenting takes place near the coast or in similarly attractive inland areas near water. How the houses are chosen I do not know, but I assume it to be from the typical process of journalistic networking and editorial judgment.

I was trained at Yale School of Architecture, where I came under the influence of the historian Vincent Scully. In his book *American Architecture and Urbanism,* he described the settings of late nineteenth-century New England summer cottages "…the coasts of Massachusetts and Maine, where the great houses weather silver, floating likes dreams of forever in the cool fogs off the sea.…" That, together with my love for the mountains and lakes of the Rangeley region, where I long ago built a "camp" for my family, led me to settle permanently in Maine and to try to design houses that embodied Scully's "dreams of forever."

As I came to know my new state over the years, primarily by driving its roads and helping people make changes to existing houses, I learned to value the lessons of the original builders, who knew about placing a house carefully on its site and about keeping it in proportion to its neighbors and its place. These were not academic lessons about form following function, or lessons about styles and periods, but a deeper sense of rightness, of careful thought expressed in careful building.

One of the best expressions of this understanding was written in 1888 by the historian and critic Marianna Griswold Van Rensselaer in her biography of the Boston architect Henry Hobson Richardson. Richardson's country

Right — *Grand Federal houses line the streets of Castine.* **Below** — *Simple clapboard boxes fit into the woods of Little Deer Isle.* **Opposite** — *The extended farmhouse—"big house, little house; back house, barn"—is the most typical Maine farm. This one is in East Machias.*

Above — *This house in Winterport combines a Greek Revival door-way with whimsical Gothic gingerbread "bargeboards."* **Opposite** — *The "paralyso" on North Haven was a summer clubhouse with apartments above. The casual design seems to have "just happened" but to be entirely appropriate in form and material.*

houses are considered the prototype of what Scully defined as the "Shingle-Style" cottages, and Van Rensselaer described one of them—the house for Reverend Percy Browne of Marion, Massachusetts— this way:

> Its foundations follow with delightful frank-
> ness the variations of the grounds upon
> which it stands, while its good proportions
> and the harmonious arrangement of its
> rooflines give it that truly architectural char-
> acter in which dignity may lie for the most
> modest building. It is so appropriate to its
> surroundings that it seems to have grown out
> of them by some process of nature, and it is
> equally appropriate to its purpose. It explains
> itself at once as a gentleman's summer
> home, but with a simplicity that does not put
> the humblest village neighbor out of counte-
> nance. Inside, the planning gives an unex-
> pected amount of comfort and air of space.
> The doorways are very wide, and are so

arranged as to afford a diagonal instead of a straight perspective. The windows are carefully placed to command every possible point of outlook, the rear views toward woods and sunset being as much considered as those that face the sea. The longer one studies this little house the better one likes it, the more typical it seems of that sort of excellence which the American owner so often craves— artistic treatment combined with cheapness, comfort with small dimensions, beauty with simplicity, refinement without decoration. Outside, the only touch of ornament is given by the varied shaping of the shingles, and inside, pleasant tints alone relieve the

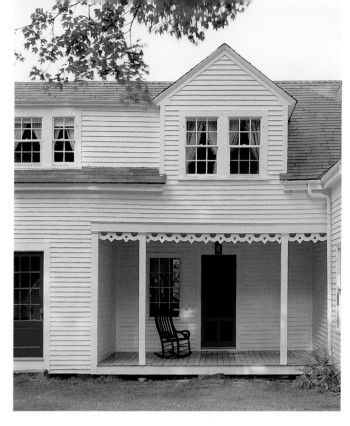

Right — *A vernacular cottage on North Haven has a little lace showing.* **Below** — *The formal fronts of a Cape and an Italianate town house are good citizens on Wiscasset's main street.* **Opposite** — *In Caratunk, a gable-ended house has acquired a front porch. Porches help relate the house to the front yard and the street.*

plainness of the woodwork, and good outlines the severity of the chimney-pieces. It has sometimes been said that Richardson took so much interest in great problems that he had none left to give to the small ones. But no one could have more carefully studied a little house like this, the cost of which, exclusive of foundations, barely exceeded twenty-five hundred dollars.

This astonishing paragraph from 1888 foreshadows many of the best twentieth-century design principles and has long served me as a touchstone for judging the success of a design. Think of the many ornate Victorian houses being built as Van Rensselaer wrote this, and think how different from them is the house she described, offering as it does simplicity, reticence, comfort, and air of space

—with small dimensions. But her first criteria are "good proportions" and a "harmonious arrangement of rooflines" and the all-important appropriateness to its surroundings, growing as if "by some process of nature." The same year Van Rensselaer wrote this, Frank Lloyd Wright was apprenticing to the builder of his family's shingle-style chapel in Wisconsin. The principles he would advocate over the course of his whole long life are here enunciated, but with a modesty and directness Mr. Wright never achieved.

As we look at the houses that follow, I will point out how they follow the criteria Mrs. Van Rensselaer extracted from Richardson's work; where they don't, I will indicate that, as well. I should mention that there are some types that are not to be found in the pages that follow. For example, with a couple of exceptions, the houses are

Previous pages — *Cottages line the shore and peek from the trees in Little Deer Isle.* **Below** — *In Aroostook, the buildings of a farm huddle close together amid the treeless fields as if to give each other shelter from the winds.* **Opposite** — *This Gothic fantasy in Friendship makes the surrounding woods an actor in a performance of* Hansel and Gretel.

Above — *Sheepscot is one of the best preserved villages in Maine: fields, woods, houses, and barns, with the church steeple uniting the whole.* *Below* — *Another view of Stonington, tightly clustered on the edge of the sea.* *Opposite* — *A sea view from a cottage porch in North Haven.*

relatively small. Sarah Susanka's excellent books on the "Not-So-Big House" have drawn attention to the desirability of the smaller house, both in terms of practicality and what Mrs. Van Rensselaer calls its "reticence." Such a dwelling uses fewer resources, is easier and less expensive to maintain and operate, and occupies a smaller "footprint" on the land. So the new generation of opulent showplace houses—the new Victorians—will not be found here.

Nor will the great historic houses of Maine. As I reviewed the houses in Brian Vanden Brink's *Down East* portfolio, I saw that the magazine had published most of the great houses, but precisely because of their greatness they were generally not appropriate to the theme of this book. Many were showplaces, where political or economic

Previous pages — *The tidal reaches of the Damariscotta River in Walpole are home to some small "camps" and, across the way, to a "cottage."* **Above** — *Castine preserves some of the best houses in a village setting little changed in a century.* **Opposite** — *Franklin Roosevelt's cottage in Campobello isn't technically in Maine, but it looks across at the Pine Tree State.*

success could be proclaimed through architecture that was extravagant—at least for Maine. Such masterpieces as the Morse-Libby house in Portland or the Hamilton house in South Berwick are not typical of the average Maine house and are probably not good models for us as we think how to build today. Those houses need a book unto themselves.

And you will not find high-tech "green" houses here, unless their green machinery is disciplined within a whole, harmonious building. I do not believe that energy efficiency is an adequate substitute for good design. The techniques of solar orientation and of planning for the seasons are as old as history, and the best houses have always employed them. Buildings that celebrate new technologies like solar panels and wind generators are valuable as experiments, but unless the technologies are subordinated to the need for appropriateness, the houses will not achieve that all-important character of fitness. We are connected to and responsible for our environment in ways that far exceed just applying the newest technological gadgets or materials, and our houses must express that.

I should say a word about architects. Unlike the majority of houses being built today, most of the houses in this book are designed by architects. Architects often have a reputation for making houses cost more, and certainly the added cost of the design work can be avoided by using a stock plan or buying a developer's model. I believe that what the architect adds to the value of the house is precisely that sense of proportion and fitness that I have been describing. The architect brings a lifetime of paying attention to these matters to bear on the problem of designing the house to fit the site, and is responsible not just for providing the client with a house that fits his needs, but one that fits the natural and cultural environment. Perhaps a good expression of the architect's approach is what Richardson himself guaranteed his clients:

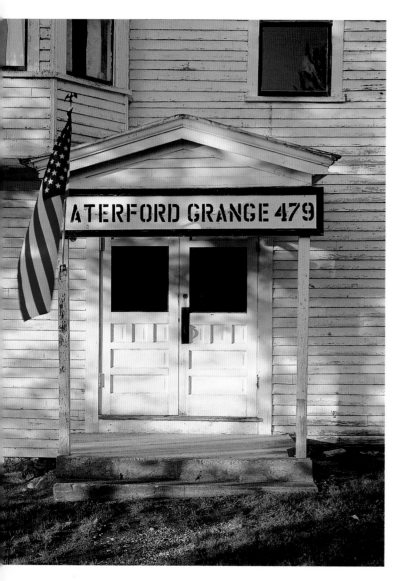

Above — *Another rural landmark is the local Grange hall. Many of these are being abandoned and might make good houses.*

Opposite — *In Little Machias, a classic cape in the quintessential Maine seascape.*

In preparing the architectural design, I agree, after consultation with the owner, to use my best judgment. I cannot, however, guarantee that the building, when completed, shall conform to his ideas of beauty or taste, or indeed to those of any person or school. I can only agree to examine and consider this matter well and carefully, and to recommend nothing which is inconsistent with my own ideas upon these subjects.

I believe the houses that follow will demonstrate the level of consideration that Richardson promised his clients, and that this level of consideration is one we should all strive to achieve, however modest our building projects.

The houses are grouped into a few categories. First are older houses adapted for contemporary use. The adaptations range from rebuilding the house from a ruined frame to doing little but refurnishing it. Next there are several examples of other building types converted to houses. Finally there are new houses on new sites built in a variety of materials and styles. All, I believe, are appropriate to Maine's history and environment.

Opposite left— A Mansard house in East Machias seems to be returning to the woods. ***Below left—*** Edward Hopper immortalized the Mansard style with his ironic **House by the Railroad** of 1925, an aristocratic house in a working-class setting. ***Above —*** More at home in its landscape is this extended Cape in Harpswell.

Preceding pages — *Another icon of Maine is the Olsen House in Cushing, immortalized in Andrew Wyeth's* Christina's World. ***Above*** — *A Maine house typically has good proportions and only enough decorative trim to show that the owner didn't skimp too much on the cost. This gable-end town house sits on its tidy lawn in Camden.*

Part Two
RENOVATING OLDER HOUSES

We will begin our survey with the best way of minimizing the impact on the land. Instead of "building new," the owners of the first set of houses rebuilt or renovated existing houses. Not only does this avoid taking a bit of the natural environment and turning it into a new, manmade artifact, but it allows houses that have had their own history and contained the lives of generations of previous Mainers to continue their usefulness into the future. Many old houses in Maine were allowed to fall into ruin because they were out of date or out of fashion—or simply too out of the way. One positive result of the access provided by the car, improved roads, and the Internet "highway" is that some of these inconveniently located houses can now be brought back to life for new owners.

The saddest aspect of our new mobility is the increasing practice of buying an old house and tearing it down to make way for a new one. All too often, especially along the Maine coast, we see good, substantial houses with a long history and graceful design bulldozed because the owners want bigger and, supposedly, better houses. This practice is contrary to the old adage "use it up and wear it out; make it do or do without," which has governed life here since before Maine was a state. It is more the way of the city, where tearing down and rebuilding are more of a necessity—though even in urban settings, new buildings are not always improvements on the old. Regrettably, one of the adages in Aldous Huxley's *Brave New World* has become part of national philosophy: "Ending is better than mending," and we are only slowly and partially unlearning it in favor of the earlier attitudes of thrift and restraint. Recycling applies not only to garbage; it also applies to buildings. The builders, renovators, and owners of the houses in our first group are to be commended for working with existing buildings to "make them do."

Nothing is more appropriate to Maine's landscape than the lakeside camp. See p. 72.

Angier House, Sheepscot

Our first example is the most typical design in Maine or New England—the Cape. It's called a Cape because there were many surviving examples on Cape Cod when scholars began to develop the language of house styles in the late nineteenth century. It featured one story and an attic for bedrooms, with a front door in the center of the eave side, and it was often connected through an ell to sheds and barns. The Cape was the most dominant design for over a century, and it has never entirely gone away, since it remains the kernel of most "Colonial" houses today. In its classic New England form, it has a massive central chimney with fireplaces on two or even three sides and a tiny winding staircase inside the front door. Later, as smaller fireplaces and cast-iron stoves were developed, the chimney moved out of the center to make room for a better staircase.

The Cape was the ideal energy-efficient building envelope. Nearly square in plan with a relatively steep

Left —The Angier house has the classic lines of a Cape, the most common and characteristic New England house. *Top* —This interior, though new, recreates a traditional Cape interior, with wide-paneled wood walls and stenciled plaster. *Above* — The kitchen ell exposes beams the original builders would have been at pains to conceal. The stove and sink would have been proud possessions, though.

roof, it approached the most efficient shape—the sphere—and it was centered on its heat source. There was only the tiny front hall, which also acted as an air-lock for the rooms, so little space was lost to hallways and passages. The upper bedchambers often had no heat, or at most a hole in the floor to allow a bit of air from below to warm but not overheat the bedrooms. Often, an ell extended off the rear, closed off in the winter but used in the summer as a kitchen, when the cross-ventilation from windows on both sides of the room cooled the cooking process. In the winter, the central kitchen fireplace or, later, the range provided the principal heat for the whole house. In Maine, the obverse of Harry Truman's advice was the rule: "If you can't stand the cold, move into the kitchen." We may tout energy efficiency today, but we are far away from the reality of keeping warm by the kitchen fire, even if we live by wood-burning furnaces in the basement. The Cape was the most direct response to dealing with the exigencies of the Maine winter.

One way to tell a real Cape from a modern adaptation is to compare their roof pitches. Capes were based on farm cottages from the British Isles, and early examples there can still be seen in the Irish and Scottish crofters'

Left — *Muted colors and light walls characterized early interiors; wide-plank floors were often unfinished and sanded.* **Above:** *the heavy frame system shows in the exposed corner post and ceiling beam. Windows were different combinations of same-sized panes.*

cottages. These most often had thatched roofs, and the pitch of the roof was the angle necessary for the thatch to shed the rain: any flatter and too much water was absorbed, working its way into the house. The walls were stone and therefore no higher than they needed to be, and the thatch started right above the windows.

In New England, a country more of forest than fen and meadow, shingles were soon substituted for thatch, but the roof angle had to be increased to prevent rain from being blown up between shingle courses. The shingles were still laid as thatch was, on open strapping nailed to the rafters, and the roof started where the thatch had, right above the windows. By the nineteenth century, the roof was more often completely boarded, and the shingles were machine sawn instead of split. As a result, they fit together better, so the angle of the roof

could be made less steep and still be watertight. Builders then raised the side walls to regain the living space lost by lowering the roof pitch. In the twentieth century, asphalt shingles replaced wood, with tar paper under the asphalt, so the pitch could be even flatter.

Carpenters measure roof pitch in what they call "rise over run," which means the number of inches of vertical rise in a foot of horizontal run. Early Capes had a pitch of ten or twelve inches per foot, with twelve inches being "square pitch," or forty-five degrees. Nineteenth-century Capes would reduce that to eight or nine inches. By the end of the twentieth century, roof pitch was down to four or five inches, with the latter being the ratio most recommended by shingle manufacturers, who didn't want their roofs to leak too soon. In general, then, the steeper the roof pitch, the older a Cape is. By "reading"

Above left — *The steep stairway saved space while avoiding the central chimney.* ***Above right***— *A sense of larger space resulted from rooms opening into each other around the chimney.* ***Opposite*** — *Of course, certain accommodations to modern taste, like interior plumbing, are usually desirable.*

the pitch you can see what period of history the roof either belongs to or aspires to.

This example, in Sheepscot, has what looks like a ten in twelve pitch. The house is unusual in that it is a reconstructed Cape made from the frames and bits of three old Capes. When in 1986 Fred and Hope Angier were offered an old Cape that "had the right lines," as a boatbuilder might say, they used it—along with two others, one for the ell and another for spare parts. So even though this house is "new," it has the proportions of the original, and it incorporates the pieces of the old.

It would have been better in the ideal world to have rebuilt the three houses where they stood, but they likely would have continued to deteriorate, and they were not located where the Angiers wanted to build. Moving and remodeling houses, however, is not a new idea. Before the advent of overhead wires made moving houses an expensive proposition, buildings of every size were picked up and hauled by oxen or trucks or even barges from one site to another, and one small house was often pushed up against another to add space without tearing

down a perfectly good frame. Now that roads and utility wires and traffic and permits have proliferated, it is harder than it used to be to move houses, and as a result we are losing more than we used to.

Inside, the rooms of the Angier house have the appearance of historic dwellings from the early nineteenth century—plastered walls, with wood wainscoting in important rooms. The wonderful hewn beams that are characteristic of these early frames are concealed by plaster. Back then, no one wanted to look at hewn beams any more than we want to look at two-by-fours and plywood today. So the kitchen ceiling of exposed beams is a modern fashion the original builders would not have understood.

Even though this is not a real "old house," it gives us a good look at that most characteristic of designs that fit the Maine landscape, and its owners are to be commended for the care with which they created it.

Poore House, Standish

Rick Poore

Historically, the next stage beyond the Cape was the two-story symmetrical house we identify as the typical "Colonial," since its architectural antecedents were the country houses built in England in the eighteenth century and widely published in pattern books used by builders in the colonies. Since the English kings during the period were the first of the Georges, the style is also called "Georgian." And the inspiration for the style came from the work of the Italian architect Andrea Palladio,

who based his designs on lessons he had derived from studies of Roman antiquity. What we call Colonial, then, represented an architecture with international origins.

This house, like the Angier Cape, was reconstructed from original frames on a new site and was finished in keeping with early practice. The reserved exterior detail, highlighted only by the formal front door; the steep stairs made necessary by the massive central chimney; the wide plank wainscoting; the wide pine floorboards,

Opposite — *Sitting in its small clearing by a pond, the Poore house embodies the best traditions of locating a house in harmony with its natural environment.* **Top left** — *Classical details connect this remote frontier with the heart of English culture.* **Top right** — *A sawbuck table complements the rough beams.* **Above** — *Base cabinets without upper cabinets help the modern kitchen respect the original architecture. Kitchen cabinets were an invention of the mid-19th century.*

Above — *The summer beam and great hearth were features of kitchen ells.* **Right** — *The near wing shows the saltbox profile: two stories on one side, sloping down to the first-floor height. This is also called a "cat slide" roof.*

sometimes painted—as in the hall—but often left bare and cleaned with fine sand; all belong to the period of the house's original construction. In the kitchen the beaded edge of the main "summer" beam indicates that in this informal room the ceiling would have been left exposed, even though the formal dining room and parlor would have had plaster ceilings. "Summer" in this context, by the way, has nothing to do with the season; it is a corruption of "sumpter," a French word, one of whose meanings is "pack horse" or "load carrier."

What this house shows especially well, though, is the

relationship of the house to its surroundings. Close up, it sits on its lawn, carefully separated from woods or shade trees or even ornamental plantings. From a distance, though, the house and its clearing seem to nestle into the woods. Seen from across the pond, it has the look of a picturesquely sited architectural element in an artfully composed landscape. This is very much what landscape architects like Lancelot "Capability" Brown were doing on country estates in England. Formal garden beds and evenly spaced rows of trees were rejected in favor of landscapes that seemed "natural."

Opposite — *The kitchen often had wood paneling, while plaster was reserved for more formal rooms.* **Left** — *Classical detail in the formal rooms proclaimed wealth and, what was more important, style.* **Below left** — *The steep stairway has an ornamental baluster with a closed stringer, even though other parts like the door were purely functional. The painted floor in the entry was an easily maintained way to protect a heavily traveled pathway.* **Below Right** — *Pantries were more usual than cabinets for kitchen storage.*

In America, where farms and towns were carved out of the unhewn forest, such a setting was by necessity more common than in agricultural England, but the new English fashion made it permissible for our environment to be developed in a way that followed the natural contours of the land and seemed less of an imposition on the environment than its Roman antecedents. Today, the careful placement of a new house on its site, even if the structure is as strict and formal a reproduction as the Poore house, can make the difference between a harmonious result and one that looks simply accidental. It is not just the house that has to be carefully considered; it is the total design of the house in its place.

Donham House, Head Tide

Brett Donham

The structure that Brett Donham restored in Head Tide represents the next phase in the evolution of the house in Maine: the two-story, hipped box. This particular one started life in 1790 as a Cape, but in 1805 a second story was added. Instead of the typical steep gable roof, however, it had the low-pitched hip roof recommended by the English "builders' assistant" handbooks and their American imitators. Though this configuration didn't work well in snowy Maine (these houses often had

steeper roofs added), the houses looked like homes of the English "gentry" rather than the "cottagers." As a result, they became more fashionable, even if the roof didn't shed the snow.

The style has different names, depending on when the houses were built and what decorative language was being used at the time. This house is called "Federal," meaning that it is from the period after the Revolution, when the United States adopted the Federal Constitution.

Nothing built after 1776 should properly be called "Colonial," even though it took a while for architectural details to evolve into something noticeably different. One difference from the Capes was that the center chimney disappeared in favor of a central stair hall. Herman Melville wrote a story called "I and My Chimney," which describes the struggles of a New England farmer trying to prevent his wife from tearing out the great center chimney in the family farm and replacing it with a grand staircase. The story shows the cultural shift that the move indicated, away from the idea of the central warming hearth and toward the stylishness of the grand hall, placing individual fireplaces to fit the rooms, rather than deploying the rooms around a single fireplace.

Brett Donham is the Boston architect who bought and restored this particular Federal in 1999. He says, "Maine had an influence on my instincts as an architect. I like spare, proportion-based architecture, where each element has a comfortable, ordered relationship—windows to walls, for example—instead of decorative, frou-frou architecture." Donham also liked the fact that this house was on the edge of Head Tide, a tiny community that preserves its village scale instead of sprawling down the highway as so many mid-coast Maine communities tend to do. Harrigan Restoration of Alna did the work of repairing the roof and cornice, and restoring the doors and windows. The exterior was returned to a condition more like its original state, though it is not true that all early buildings were white.

On the inside, Donham opened the rooms to create a large living and dining space unlike what would have been considered proper by the original builders. If there is one defining difference between today's house planners and those of the last century, it is the former's increased desire for open space—what Mrs. Van Rensselaer presciently referred to as "an unexpected amount of comfort and air of space." Early houses tended toward multiple small special-purpose rooms for reasons not only of heating economy but also of a greater desire for separating activities such as eating or reading or socializing. Then, too, many more houses had at least part-time servants. In the late twentieth century, we have seen the return to the medieval model of the "great room," the extended multipurpose space that allows us a large area in a small house by eliminating the separation of dining rooms and living rooms and

Opposite — *The Donham house is a classical box on a flat site carved from a sloping hill. Note the smaller upstairs windows with fewer panes of the same size as those in the lower windows.* **Left** — *A modern addition extends the original box.* **Right** — *The stair's dadoed paneling added style while protecting the walls.*

kitchens. The Donham house shows how this can be done within a historic structure while still keeping the character of the original.

Donham's other significant departure from the expectations of the exterior is to furnish the interior not with period antiques or reproductions but with examples of the best of modern design. Of course, putting Federal furniture in a Federal house is a sign of respect for the builders, but it can equally be argued that bringing in good contemporary work is a way of saying that both styles embody good design and good craftsmanship, and that their common excellence is more significant than their differing centuries. Donham says, "The furnishings and the house have an affinity. They're both spare, well proportioned, and simple. It's what a teacher of mine called a 'bicycle aesthetic.' It's very handsome, but also very purposeful and intentional. Every element clearly has its purpose."

Before the nineteenth century invented the idea of copying historic styles for their cultural associations, the basic principle of good design was correct proportion, which meant that the sizes and location of different building elements like windows and columns—even the whole exterior shape of the building—followed rules said to be derived from classical theories of mathematical relationships between objects. Though there were lots of specific versions of the theory, many of which contradicted each other, there was a consensus that architectural beauty derived from these relationships. Moreover, the consensus held that it was just as unnecessary to be aware of the mathematics to appreciate architectural beauty as it was to understand musical theory in order to enjoy music. Architects studied proportion to be able to create works that appealed to deep and real laws of beauty, laws that applied to the human body and to trees and

Above and opposite below — *The interiors contrast the exposed beams and traditional paneling with modern furnishings, creating a dialog across the generations.* **Opposite above** — *The house, nestled beneath the church, in the tiny village of Head Tide.*

landscapes, as well as buildings. A house whose dimensions followed these rules was more correct, and therefore more beautiful, than a house that ignored them. Several modern architects, notably the Swiss designer Le Corbusier, have tried to combine classical proportion theory with a modern functionalist design language, and architects less committed to functionalism have sought to reintroduce classical design theory in order to correct what they see as the visual chaos of modernism. Donham's house, with its modernist interior inside a classical shell, is a good example of this continuing dialog.

Howe Hill Farm, Camden

Scholz and Barclay

A similar love for the land and the house on it led architects John Scholz and Meg Barclay to buy and renovate the Walter Howe farm on Howe Hill, outside of Camden. The farmhouse dates only from 1907, but it has the classic lines of the architecture that evolved over the nineteenth century from the many stylistic waves washing over our shores from Europe. Turning the roof so that the gable faced the street (whereby snow from the roof wouldn't pile up on the doorstep) was an idea that came

originally from what is known as the Greek Revival. During this period, houses tried to look like Greek temples to honor the birthplace of democracy and thereby emphatically declare our architectural independence from England—though England had its own Greek Revival. Then long porches were introduced and called "piazzas" in reference to similar features of northern Italian villas. Our houses became miniature world tours.

By 1907, there was a pretty well-established vernacular

architecture of houses, still featuring relatively steep roofs, knee walls upstairs for headroom in the bedrooms, and a long kitchen ell, often with an open or windowed porch. The ell sometimes connected through sheds to the barn, often in an unplanned cluster of pieces added over the years.

Scholz and Barclay chose to keep the exterior of the Howe house essentially unchanged on the exterior, except for enhancing the ell with a gable dormer that mimicked one that was already there. A few new windows that kept the same layout and proportions were tucked into spaces between the original windows, and the existing ell porch was lengthened. All these changes were done in a way that respected the architectural "language" of the original house.

Inside, the changes included building new bathrooms (the house had no running water when they bought it in 1993) and opening up the downstairs but leaving partial partitions and screens to identify separate spaces within the open area. New work was done using techniques and materials consistent with the time of the house's original construction, and the effect is one of a new kind of space—but in the style of the original.

There is a difference of opinion among those interested in historic preservation. Some believe that any changes made to an existing building should be clearly different so that they cannot be confused with the original work, while others think that it is more important for

Opposite — *This "vernacular farmhouse" appears unchanged from the time of its construction, but the interior (below) shows how the spaces have been modified to today's open plan.*

Opposite — *The house and its barn sit above the home pasture. A new stone terrace betrays a more leisured life than the farm family would have led.* ***Above*** — *Eclectic furnishings and period plumbing fixtures connect the house to its history.*

the final building to represent a single harmonious style, meaning that additions should blend in as invisibly as possible. Generally, historians favor the former approach and architects the latter, though there are designers whose principal aim is to make their contribution as distinctive as possible. While some of my best friends are historians, I think like an architect, and I admire what I call "invisible additions" more than work that calls attention to itself. The Scholz-Barclay house is a good example of what I mean, and its harmonious presence in its preserved landscape is for me the best evidence of the soundness of the respectful approach.

In describing their approach to the process, Meg Barclay says, "We are all creatures of history. Whether we think about it or not, we all have history behind us. Those subliminal notions of home—whether pictures from books or from our parents' house—get triggered when we're in an old place, and we feel comfortable. I prefer to see myself as part of a continuum rather than living in a house that dropped out of the sky in some Los Angeles suburb."

Especially on old farmland in the Camden Hills, a suburban house would look as if it had landed from outer space. One of the most important characteristics of how a house fits its site is how it relates to both its immediate surroundings and to the entire landscape visible from the house. The Scholz-Barclay house, sitting at the top of an extensive bowl of fields tucked into the higher hills and the nearer woodlands, is the quintessential upland farm. The old maples along the stone fence in front recall the tradition of planting shade trees along the roads to make driving more pleasant for people and for horses. Those trees were often sugar maples, which were more easily tapped because they could be reached from the road. Understanding the origins of these traditions makes living in the landscape a richer experience.

The area around the house is open rather than planted with shrubbery. The perimeter of the masonry foundation beneath a house is an often overlooked hole in the insulation envelope: since masonry has an insulating value about equal to glass, houses in effect sit on a window running around their entire perimeter, and a lot of heat

Below — *One of the few exterior concessions to the need for more light is a duplicate of the original ell dormer.* *Opposite* — *Farmhouses are best seen in the context of the landscape they were meant to fit—the farm.*

goes out that window during the winter. Farmhouses in Maine were traditionally "banked" during the winter with hay bales or, less commonly, rotted horse manure that would give off heat. Installing the banking in the fall and taking it out in the summer to allow the cellar to breathe required that the space around the house be left clear.

An old farmhouse tells a lot about itself by what it doesn't say. It boasts of no fancy trim, no ornamental landscaping. The house just sits among its outbuildings on land intended for producing crops, not enjoying views. In its simplicity and directness it is a model for all our houses, and we do well to study its lessons.

Yourcenar House, Northeast Harbor

Of course it should be remembered that the most respectful way of living in an old house is to make no changes to it at all. What we have seen so far are houses in which the owners have "intervened"—they have modified the houses to make them more livable according to the desires of the late twentieth century. In the case of the Northeast Harbor house that French author Marguerite Yourcenar acquired in 1950, no major changes were made. The photographs show the results of

the process we all use to make our dwelling places our own—we fill it with our own stuff. Too often today that means gadgets and high-end appliances and media centers, but the Yourcenar house, which the owner named "Petite Plaisance," is filled with things that stimulate personal memories. It is not surprising in the house of a writer that the main artifacts should be books, on shelves added wherever there was an underused space. Quirky additions done for self-evidently functional reasons,

rather than "effect," make the interior look inhabited rather than decorated.

Yourcenar was once asked why she chose to live in Northeast Harbor instead of returning to her native France, to live in Brittany. She replied, "I have my Brittany here." Looking around the rooms full of personal possessions confirms that. We all have our histories with us, and we fill our spaces with objects that remind us of who we are. We may be at home in Maine, but our houses contain evidence of the larger world that is our real home.

Outside, the Yourcenar house is a good neighbor. Like the Scholz-Barclay house, it is essentially a vernacular gable-end design with a long ell. Its steep roof had been extended down to form a "piazza" along the side, and a bay window of similar Italian origin had been added to dress up the front. In this case the house sits on a town lot in a village, and its ell porch is shaded by an arbor more typical of France than Maine. But it has not been

Opposite — *This village house reaches toward the street with a bay window, porch and grape arbor. A screened porch, is tucked under its left wing.* **Above** — *The interior spaces have been made comfortable by a profusion of familiar belongings.*

made to look "foreign"; it has just been enhanced by an unobtrusive addition that quietly differentiates it from quite similar neighbors. The conversation is polite, a chat among friends in which one friend has a slight foreign accent. Too often our streets are either boring, with very similar houses saying nothing of interest, or noisy, with showplace houses crying out for attention. The classic Maine village is like the conversation around the stove in the general store—each one says only what needs to be said, in an atmosphere of understated consensus.

Smithwick House, Boothbay Harbor

Martin Moore

This house, called Rosecliffe, is an unusual approach to renovation, because it involved taking a simple cottage from the 1920s and adding elements and details from the 1840s to make the house appear older than it really was. Owners Walter and Cornelia Covington Smithwick worked with designer Martin Moore to add porches, dormers, and period trim to create a classic Gothic Revival cottage.

The Gothic Revival was promoted as a style that

embodied both the picturesque virtues of harmony in the romantic landscape and the moral virtues of family life. The great prophet of the Gothic style in England was John Ruskin, and in America the houses that look like Rosecliffe were designed and promoted by Andrew Jackson Downing. Downing developed the ideas of Capability Brown, and he believed that the house should belong to its natural landscape, instead of sitting on it in the formal way Georgian or Federal houses did—dominating

Opposite — *A seaside cottage has been decorated and extended to recall romantic Gothic cottages from the 1850s.* **Above** — *Behind the furniture and above the rebuilt fireplace can be seen hints of the simple old cottage.* **Left** — *A Gothic arch is the appropriate frame for the garden entrance.*

the axially planned formal gardens or lawns. Natural beauty was irregular, beautiful forms grew organically, and therefore, said Downing, the house—like the landscape—should incorporate natural forms through porches and bay windows and dormers placed to take advantage of the views and to produce an irregular silhouette against the backdrop of woods and sky. Interiors should not be grander than family life required, and there should be quiet corners and cozy nooks. And the detail in the house should refer to what Downing felt was the period in which civilization reached the summit of its moral development—the Middle Ages. Like the novels of Sir Walter Scott, the literary equivalent of the Gothic cottages, such houses would celebrate and teach moral virtue.

Rosecliffe, even though it was not originally Gothic, successfully conveys these virtues. The steep roofs with

their gables and dormers provide the irregular outline, and they are trimmed with medieval "barge boards." (Here, "barge" has no nautical meaning. It is a corruption of "verge," or edge.) A porch connects the house to the sea view, and it is divided into separate areas by sweeping out into an angled bay. The furnishings recall the Gothic theme, and only occasionally—as in the simple exposed joists of the living-room ceiling—do traces of the original 1920s cottage show through. Whimsical touches like the birch handrail indicate that we are not to take Gothic authenticity too seriously.

The most Gothic aspect of the house is the treatment of the landscape, which master gardener Gail MacPhee helped the Smithwicks to shape into the romantic grouping of paths and arbors and beds that defined the new vision of the Gothic Revival. Unlike the stolid farmhouse that sits on its clearing of lawn, the Gothic cottage nestles into its leafy bower.

It can be argued that no revival style is appropriate, and that it was not appropriate in the 1840s to build houses that looked as if they belonged to the fourteenth century. But the question is not just one of being faithful to one's own time. The larger issue is how to create a living environment that enhances life, that produces feelings of

Top — *Even the kitchen has a hand in the Gothic game.* **Above** — *The luxuriant gardens "embower" the cottage as A. J. Downing recommended.* **Opposite** — *Lest the old stair look too ordinary, the handrail has been replaced by a birch trunk.*

integration with the world of nature and of society, and enables us to be better citizens of that world. The theorists of the Gothic Revival made that claim for their architecture, just as the proponents of the Shingle Style and, indeed, of modern architecture would do in their turn. We can either choose one way and reject the others, or we can ask of each house whether it lifts us up and improves the place where it sits, or whether it obtrudes on its site and depresses us to experience it.

Finally, it is not the style that matters. It is the attention to place. It is the way the building fits the land, and the way the building fits our lives and our society.

Bottom and right— The garden envelops the porch, while the rooms open to the sea. **Opposite** *— Light streams through Gothic tracery in a triangular window. This juxtaposition was characteristic of "carpenter Gothic."*

Lakeside Camp, Western Maine

Stephen Blatt

This camp was published in *Down East* with no owner's name, and the lake next to which it sits was not identified. It is a set of historic log structures dating from the early days of lakeside camp-building in Maine. At the end of the nineteenth century, inland Maine began to discover itself—first as a destination for fishermen and hunters and then for what had earlier been called "rusticators," people who wished to leave their more settled urban or suburban lives and spend some time in the woods. Of course, Henry David Thoreau had been the pioneer of this movement, with his retreat to the cabin he built himself, for $28.12, on Walden Pond. His motto was, "I went to the woods because I wished to live deliberately, to front only the essential facts of life, and see if I could not learn what it had to teach, and not, when I came to die, discover that I had not lived...."

In the 1880s Cornelia "Flyrod" Crosby of Phillips was told to get out into nature to cure her tuberculosis, and she developed a love for fishing and hunting. She wrote news of the sporting camps and was eventually hired by the Maine Central Railroad to promote sporting vacations in Maine, traveling to exhibitions in places like Madison Square Garden with log camps and stuffed bears. She worked to professionalize the fishing and hunting guides, and in honor of her efforts was awarded the first Maine Guide's license in 1897.

Sporting camps promptly sprang up throughout the Maine woods. They were roughly built from local timber, with a few windows and doors hauled in, along with the camp stove. They certainly fit the land, often moving with the frost heaves and collapsing under the wet March snows. They were never intended as permanent structures. Only in a few places in Maine do camps from the early days survive. Where they do, their owners cherish

Opposite — *This early camp has been extended with a large screened porch and a double stairway that make a graceful transition to the lawn sloping down to the lake.* *Below —* *The snug interior, features a breakfast nook between chimney and window. Note the mugs hanging from the rafters. Camp life should be informal, and the buildings should match that informality.*

Above— Wood walls and ceilings allow camps to move with the seasons without cracking plaster. *Opposite* — The casual cluster of outbuildings shows the different materials typical of camps: stacked logs, vertical logs (usually used for sheds), and the ever-handy wooden shingles. The diagonal window is of course just a square window stood on a corner. The far shed shows the kind of post footings that need "retuning" each spring.

them and put up with the yearly jacking of the support posts to persuade the doors to close again.

To make such camps a bit less rustic, many owners have added twentieth-century amenities like bathrooms and kitchens and even foundations. This camp is a good case in point. The owners had lived in it for thirty years before deciding in 1994 that it needed to be a bit more practical, especially for an extended family. They did not want to change the character of the camp, however, and the challenge for the architect was to make the needed changes without introducing elements that stood out as innovations.

A problem of old camps is that they are often not laid out in functionally practical ways. Steven Blatt and the owners rethought everything—from how the driveway arrives at the house to how the leftover space between the main structure and the bunkhouse could be turned into an outdoor courtyard by relocating an old

Top — *The kitchen is under a shed roof at the side.* **Above** — *The central gathering room around the chimney is a kind of medieval great hall—but still a camp.* **Opposite** — *A screened porch is the best transition between inside and outside.*

pantry wing. A new wing houses the kitchen and new spaces for a mudroom and office, allowing the core of the old lodge to remain untouched. Not wanting to attempt the impossible of matching new logs to the old walls, the owners shingled the new additions to match the older outbuildings.

Finally, the original open veranda was screened so it could be used at the prime mosquito-feeding hour, which always coincides with sunset over the lake. Its steep steps were changed to a less obtrusive double stair running parallel to the porch.

"The challenge," says the owner, "was getting the new additions and the original parts of the house to flow." And the architect says, "If you look closely, you can see what's new and what's old, but it isn't jarring." The emphasis in the renovation is on respect for the original and on what it stood for. The result is still manifestly a Maine camp, and its historic core is intact. On its new foundation, the structure doesn't even have to have the posts "retuned" each spring. New needs have been met without destroying the existing character of the camp, and the compound of casually placed sheds has been subtly transformed into a coherent whole—as Mrs. Van Rensselaer would say, "with a reticence that does not put the humblest village neighbor out of countenance." This is responsible stewardship of the building and its land.

Above — *The camp is organized with layers of space. You look through from one area to another toward the outside.* **Opposite** — *Though the camp has been reorganized and extended, it retains the simplicity and fitness that attracted the owners forty years ago.*

Anderson House, Camden

Christopher Glass

What should an owner do when his house is too small? Upgrade to a larger structure or expand the one he has? This is the problem that faced Richard and Sandy Anderson. In 1994 they had bought a house on Dillingham Point in Camden, but it was a small summer cottage not able to accommodate the visits of their adult children. They moved the house to the edge of the property and lived there while having a larger, Shingle Style cottage designed for the original site. But, as they became

more familiar with the old cottage, and as they looked out over the expanse of lawn where it had been and where they were planning to build, they began to have second thoughts.

The house was one of the first summer cottages built in Camden, and its design had been based on the Gothic Revival cottages being erected at summer church-meeting camps in places like Oak Bluffs on Martha's Vineyard and at Bayside, in the nearby Maine town of

Northport. These summer camps were often owned by local churches throughout the region, and parishioners could take turns living in the camps and participating in summer worship and recreation activities. Since the cottages replaced the tents on platforms that had been built first, they were tiny and close together and lacking much in the way of amenities like interior walls and, of course, plumbing. They were often sided with vertical boards and wooden strips called battens sealed the vertical joints between the boards. This siding was more often found in barns and sheds, where the fact that it didn't do a perfect job of keeping out the weather was not as important as it was in houses. Board-and-batten construction had also been hailed by the Gothic Revival guru Andrew Jackson Downing as morally purer: "We greatly prefer the vertical

*Opposite — The right-hand section is an old summer camp moved up onto the side of the hill. The center and left-hand sections extend it without overwhelming it. **Below** — The link between the old and new is a family room, lit by a skylight to brighten the otherwise dark center. **Right** — The dining room is in the old house, where the joists and studs are left exposed.*

to the horizontal boarding, not only because it is more durable, but because it has an expression of truthfulness which the other has not. The main timbers that enter into the frame of a wooden house are vertical, and hence the vertical boarding properly signifies to the eye a wooden house…. It is as incorrect, so far as regards truthfulness of construction, to show horizontal lines on the weatherboarding of a wooden wall, as it would be to mark vertical lines on the outside of a brick or stuccoed wall." In addition to its moral virtue it was also cheap.

The Andersons started renovating the original cottage by removing its board-and-batten sheathing, adding rigid insulation, and resheathing it with new pine boards and half-round battens. They put a garage under the house—tucked into its new foundation—and they added a new kitchen and bath. Otherwise, however, they left the cottage pretty much intact. But as their main house, the structure was still too small for their needs. Then in 1999 they decided to explore adding on, but they did not want to lose the scale and charm and openness of the original. That was when I was asked to take a look at the problem. (Yes, this is the one design of my own that appears in *At Home in Maine*.)

The Andersons had moved the house very near to their property line, so that it was impossible to expand up the hill, and adding on to the side meant running into a zoning setback line. I told them that the basic principle of design is the method Sherlock Holmes used to solve his cases: "When you have eliminated everything that is impossible, whatever remains, however improbable, must be the truth." In this case, that meant creating a second "house," similar in scale to the original and connected to it by a common room that allowed the original structure and the new wing to have uninterrupted views and

Below — A hallway through the old kitchen opens into the central room. *Opposite* — *A dormer in the old house is a spartan bedchamber.*

Above — *Upstairs in the new wing, crossed gables—emphasized by arched valleys—shelter a library.* **Opposite** — *From the street the original camp is little changed but is nestled in a new, informal hillside garden.*

access to an expanded porch that would anchor the house to the landscape. The new connector and wing were angled because of the need to follow the setback line, but the angle kept the complex from looking too planned and rigid. The two separate "houses" actually look more like the cheek-by-jowl Bayside cottages than did the single original.

Details of the construction were modeled on the original cottage, though the open joists and studs were not copied, since new framing wood is a good deal more processed than older two-by-fours and does not give the same sense of rawness. It's also easier to install insulation and wiring when the framing isn't exposed. Instead, the interior was sheathed in beaded and V-matched pine, for which Sandy Anderson, who is a painter, chose the carefully muted colors.

Sitting on the side of its hill, the expanded house looked larger than it actually was, and landscaper Tom

Jackson helped tie the structure to the grounds and mask its height by adding boulders and shrubs to make the surroundings look more rugged. The lawn, which was to have been the site of a new house, provides an open expanse beyond which are views to the Camden Hills and Penobscot Bay, while the house nestles into the wooded boundary on the hillside.

If the very best method of preserving an existing house (and its landscape) is to use it the way it was intended, the next best is to incorporate as much as possible of the old into the new, so that the qualities that made the old structure desirable are not lost along the way. A new owner has a responsibility to his predecessors to honor what they have bequeathed him, not just the property but the the embodied dreams a house represents. The new owner brings new visions, but those are richer and more embedded in reality to the extent that they build on the old.

Above — *Narrow vistas connect the Anderson house with the water.*

Part Three
CONVERTING OTHER BUILDINGS TO HOUSES

So far, we have been discussing examples of houses that have been modified to fit the changing needs of their owners. Now let us turn to the possibilities of taking buildings that were not intended as houses and see how new owners have adapted them as living spaces. While a historian would prefer that each structure be kept for its original use, he would nonetheless want the building to be preserved rather than destroyed. If that means putting it to a new use, at least that would be better than leaving it with no use. For the new owners there is the added delight of seeing the way the new use of the building interacts with its original purpose. A space originally meant for horses, for example, has a depth of association that one always used for domestic life does not.

A war-surplus coaling station on Little Diamond Island has become a guest cottage.

Thorn House, Bass Harbor

Christian Fasoldt with Susan Thorn

Here the original was a highly detailed horse barn. Owners Bill and Susan Thorn note, "When you look at some old barns, you find that people often treated their horses much better than they treated their help—or sometimes even their family."

This particular horse barn was actually built from mail-order plans, which can often mean that it doesn't seem to fit comfortably on its site. In this case, however, the structure seems to stand quietly enough in its meadow.

The plan was from Shoppell's Modern Houses of 1889. Shoppell was one of many publishers of plan books and magazines, and a lot of these companies were centered on lower Fifth Avenue, in the heart of New York City. Such plans gave the consistent Victorian character to houses and stores built throughout the country in the 1870s and 80s. Long before the standardization of the post-World War II suburbs, or even the bungalow communities of the 1920s, the Victorian houses spread a uniform style

Opposite — *A pattern-book carriage house has become a fanciful cottage.* **Above and below** — *Original colored glass has been left to brighten the interiors. The original sliding barn doors have been rehung inside new glass doors.*

across widely different geographies. Remember the image of the house in the middle of the Texas plains in the film version of Edna Ferber's *Giant?* Or the austere grandeur of Edward Hopper's *House by the Railroad* (page 32)?

What kept neighborhoods full of such houses from having the monotony of the fifties suburbs (or of today's suburban tracts) was the variety inherent in the designs. The draftsmen in New York seemed to compete with each other in producing new variations of bays and towers and decorative treatments, and this made for lively neighborhoods. These adventurous designs were made possible by mass production and mass transportation for materials, both of which resulted from turning the industrial machinery and railroads expanded for the Civil War to peaceful pursuits. A high point of this economy was the 1876 Centennial Exhibition in Philadelphia (a remnant of which still exists in the Smithsonian's Art and Industries Building). Here machine tools and tractors

shared space with mechanical musical instruments like the mighty Orchestrion, and Americans celebrated a century of material achievement. They were likewise inclined to show off their houses, and the machines made it possible to embellish these structures without requiring expensive craftsmanship.

So this little carriage house was originally an exercise in turning the practical into the fanciful, and the Thorns invited Camden architect Chris Fasoldt to help them keep the fanciful while making the house practical. Guiding both the designer and the owners was the Maine Historic Preservation Commission, because the Thorns chose to follow the national preservation standards that the Commission administers. The house had been listed on the National Register of Historic Places, and the Thorns wanted to preserve the option of renting it out and thus being eligible for preservation tax credits. Fasoldt says, "You have to follow the Secretary of the Interior's 'Standards and Guidelines for Historic Preservation.' It's a long list of 'dos and don'ts.' But I find it fun to see how different people at different times approached various problems. With a building, there's a certain language that's spoken, and you have to learn that language and how to speak it."

The exterior was kept intact, with glass doors filling the original stable doors, which were rehung on their sliding tracks inside the building. The original multicolored panes of glass in the windows were retained despite the loss of view. The new kitchen and bath were designed using techniques and materials in the language of the period so as not to break the consistency of the architecture. Elements from the old stalls—like the wrought-iron feed basket—were kept as reminders of the previous inhabitants.

The result is a building whose obsolescence has been solved by adapting it to the needs of a new era. The Thorns comment, "Too often we're sending our heritage to the landfill. Taking down something that is old and beautiful and has character in order to put up something new and made of plastic—it's tragic."

Top — *View from the dinning area to the living room.* **Above** — *A close-up of the colored window shows how the clear panes give a glimpse of the outside.* **Opposite** — *Hay grates from the stalls appropriately decorate the dining area.*

Converted Barn, Westport Island

Just as stables are now generally obsolete, so also are most house barns, which used to be the place the family's horse and cow and chickens were kept, even if the family was not in the business of farming. Ordinances now frequently prevent the keeping of animals other than pets, and cars, of course, have replaced horses as our means of transportation. Garages have no haylofts overhead and so do not have the same volume as the barns they have replaced. When a barn is still part of a house, it is often converted to a living area that takes advantage of the vertical space afforded by the shape of the structure.

The most exciting part of a barn is its frame, the heavy timbers that support the hayloft and roof. Barns represent the survival of the kind of construction that preceded the invention in the 1830s of the "balloon frame" of two-by-fours nailed together to form walls as light and taut as the skin of a balloon. This is the system that, with small variations, has been used ever since for

house construction. In timber framing, individual timbers are shaped for their specific places in the frame, and careful joints are carved to allow them to fit together without metal hardware. This is one reason barns can be taken down and reassembled more easily than other buildings. "Frames," or sets of posts and beams in a single plane across the width of the barn, are assembled flat on the floor and raised, originally by hand, by a gang using long "gin poles" to support the ends of the frame as it is tilted up into place, where it is locked to the other frames by the beams that run parallel to the ridge line. Boards, often unplaned, are then nailed—usually vertically—to the framing members.

Barns still in use typically only have one or two open "bays" (the space defined by four posts) for hauling hay to the loft above the main floor, but the temptation to open up more such bays to achieve interior height is nearly irresistible. Once the owner sees the frame before

Opposite — *The barn completes the composition of connected structures. Its windows show respect for traditional patterns on the side, and a dramatic modern gesture on the end toward the view of the lighthouse (left and below).*

the loft floor is closed off, it is hard to give up the great, open interior—even though a farmer would wonder why all that space was being wasted.

Of course, barns don't have much in the way of windows or even insulation in the walls. The problem for anyone converting a barn to a house is the question of those exterior walls—how to insulate them and how to place windows that still keep the character of the barn. If the original frame and typical barn boards are to show on the inside, any insulation has to be applied outside the sheathing, with a new exterior skin applied over the insulation on both the roof and sidewalls. Since the roof shingles and sidewall shingles (or clapboards) are usually in need of replacement, it is better to change them than to abandon the interior boarding. Placing windows is trickier, because the braced frame allows few convenient locations.

The example here is an old house-and-barn frame erected as a new house. The owners bought a Shaker

Right and Below — *The reassembled frames define the spaces in the house as well as in the barn.* **Opposite** — *Even with its modern window the barn fits well with the other shapes, and they all follow the natural shape of the shoreline.*

barn in Vermont, without knowing where they would eventually use it. Around 1990 they decided to put it on Southport Island, and Wiscasset architect Paul Bruno Mrozinski helped them add it to a Cape frame they had also acquired. The barn is one large open space, with small vents in the peak toward the ell, high windows along one side, traditionally divided windows on the other side, but three large, undivided windows facing the lighthouse on the point. The exterior is sheathed in vertical boards (in contrast to the shingles of the main house), and this use of materials recreates the hierarchy of finish that was scrupulously observed in older complexes: stone was more important than brick, brick than clapboard,

clapboard than shingle, shingle than vertical siding. Using clapboard on a barn connected to a shingled house would have been a social faux pas. Inside, the framing members are prominent, with only the floor joists that would have interrupted the main window left out. The resulting space is high and generous, but without the formality of the great rooms of the new breed of Victorian mansions.

The complex of house, ell, and barn break down a large house into a cluster of smaller buildings that seem less imposing on the exposed site than a single structure of the same volume. The tradition of connected, houses —sometimes described as—"big house, little house, back

Above — *The elements are placed to seem added together rather than planned as a whole. That takes careful planning.* **Opposite** — *The floor beam and some floor joists have been kept, but the loft floor has not. The notches show where other joists used to be.*

house, barn"—is strong in Maine, as it is elsewhere in New England. Often house and barn were built separately, and then the connections were added, with the result looking as if it had grown organically—as in fact it had. The variety of sizes, openings, and siding materials gives these complexes an accidental quality that in itself makes them seem less pompous or dominating. The different elements are just doing their different jobs.

The business of relocating existing barn frames has been supplemented in recent years by the rediscovery of timber-frame joinery techniques. Numerous builders now create barn frames, more generically called post-and-beam frames, to fit new structures of all kinds. The frame is exposed inside the building, as it is in a barn, and the exterior walls are applied to the frame, often as pre-insulated panels. This kind of construction can be more weathertight and structurally stronger than conventional "stick-built" construction, as the successors to balloon frames are called. It is usually more expensive, however,

and it presents the problems of adding wiring and plumbing that can be run in the wall cavities of conventional buildings. The character of the heavy timbers and the care evident in the craftsmanship of the joinery are, for many people, worth the additional expense. The post-and-beam structures relate the interior to the natural environment of the exterior, in effect helping to "bring the outside in."

But a real barn, with its solid bulk looming up over the fields surrounding it, has the scale and historic association that makes it seem to belong on the land without the softening concession of dormers or ells or porches. While timber framing is a construction technique that can be applied to any house, a real barn frame imposes the geometrical logic of its construction on its shape, and its shape is the essential terminus of the traditional connected house, whether it is a saltwater farm on the edge of the sea or a house in the village.

Coaling Station , Little Diamond Island

Rob Whitten

What barns are to agricultural Maine, boathouses are to the coast. Today's shoreland zoning assumes that new buildings are private houses with no necessary connection to the water and thus restricts their location to at least seventy-five feet from the water's edge. Mainers, however, have long regarded the water not just as a scenic attraction but a terrain to be worked—like a farm—to produce an income, and historically the most common buildings along the water's edge have been utilitarian.

Boathouses, fishing shacks and canneries, sail and rope lofts, the famous lighthouses—these simple structures define the Maine coast far more accurately than even the best integrated summer cottage or saltwater farmhouse.

The reality of Maine's modern economy and marine technology, however, is that most such buildings are no longer needed. With trucks and trailers, boats can be stored and worked on anywhere. Fish can be processed at sea and taken directly to market. Coast Guard stations

Opposite — *A former Coast Guard refueling shed sits on the wharf at Little Diamond Island, little changed except for added windows.*

Above — *The utilitarian interior has been left exposed.*

have been consolidated. The decline of the inshore fisheries and the dramatic rise in the value of shore frontage mean that it is no longer financially possible to devote shoreline to such humble uses. As with farms and villages, the traditional coastal fishing harbor is disappearing from the Maine coast.

Occasionally, though, one of these buildings finds a sympathetic owner, and this little boathouse had that good fortune. One of three built by the Coast Guard during World War II as refueling stops for boats that maintained anti-submarine nets in Casco Bay, it had a postwar career as a small store and center for summer activities. The owners described it as "the best place for a party" on the island. When they gave up running the store, they sold it to a developer, whose ambitious plans for the property fell through. That provided an opportunity for the present

Right and Opposite — *Diagonal beams meant purely for wind bracing join the rafters exposed by the new dormer to create dramatic patterns in the space.* **Below** — *On the outside the simple, clean lines give little hint of the drama inside.*

NO SMOKING

Opposite — *A row of windows, interrupted only by the bracing, brings the sea view in, while the sliding doors (above) literally open the living room to the wharf.*

owner to turn the place into what it is today: a boathouse to which only a few amenities were added in order to enable it to be lived in. This is not a case, as we see too frequently, of using the preexisting building as an excuse for building something new and fancy instead of renovating the modest original. Architect Rob Whitten respected the simplicity and soundness of the existing structure; he used materials and details and, more important, a strong sense of design restraint to keep the appearance and feeling of the original boathouse.

The exterior is untreated cedar shingles that will weather naturally. Windows, even in the new dormers, have the small panes of barn sash typical of the old building. Inside, the structural frame and board walls have simply been painted white, while the roof boards have been left natural. The loft has been opened up into a single space—something that the Coast Guard would have

thought inefficient but which makes the small building less claustrophobic. Where most owners would have wanted sliding doors and large windows, the opening toward the water is a sliding barn door, which—whether open or closed—retains the appearance of a functioning boathouse.

It can be argued that converting buildings like barns and boathouses to houses fundamentally alters their relationship to the land, just as converting working farms to suburban estates does. That is true, but it is also true that without such conversions the buildings would likely decay and be demolished, and our landscape and history would be the poorer for their loss. Even changed into summer houses, they still preserve an echo of their original purpose and still grace our land with their presence. Those who choose to preserve them by converting them deserve our gratitude.

Kragsyde, the Beyor and Goodrich House, Swan's Island

Before we move on to new designs, here is a Maine house that is neither a restoration nor a conversion. It is, however, a dramatic example of the owners' love for the values of a historic dwelling. Builders of new houses always have the option of copying an existing design, and developers reproduce successful models by the hundreds. Seldom, however, do house builders try to recreate a house of the complexity and historic importance of Kragsyde.

The original Kragsyde was designed in 1882 by the Boston firm of Peabody and Stearns for a site in Manchester-by-the-Sea, Massachusetts. Because it was such an icon of the architectural style that historian Vincent Scully named the Shingle Style, he used it on the cover of his book on the period, and that's where Jane Goodrich first saw it as a young girl. When in 1982 she and her husband James Beyor decided to build on Swan's Island, they visited Kragsyde for inspiration and learned that it had been demolished. But the original plans still

existed in the archives of the local public library. They decided to recreate it.

What made this possible was that Beyor was a builder and collector of historic building materials. Rather than hire architects and consultants, he could build the house himself from the plans, using period materials where they resembled those called for on the drawings. Even though Goodrich and Beyor built from the original plans, they used modern techniques, so that the result is more an homage to Kragsyde than a replica. They even decided to reverse the plan to fit their site better. This would probably have been approved by Peabody and Stearns, since their design was based on the outcropping of rock on the original Massachusetts site. The house is actually quite large, but the essence of the Shingle Style is that the buildings seem to grow out of their surroundings rather than dominating them. The angles of the plan, the roof planes that come down low over the windows, and—above all—the shaggy coat of weathered shingles, all make even a large house appear at home in its environment. Kragsyde nestles into the trees and the rocks, and its

Opposite — Though hardly a humble cottage, this house shows how even a large stucture can almost disappear into its environment.
Top — The richly detailed interior is concealed within the shaggy, shingled exterior. The two meet on the porches (above).

Opposite — *Simple materials used with care keep this monumental entry from excessive opulence.* *Above* — *The interiors recall 18th-century predecessors.*

rooms open out to porches and terraces that can seem more like tree houses than formal living space.

Even though this is not a house everyone could aspire to, the lessons of its design can be applied to more modest projects. One of those lessons is to look at history —but to look critically: Choose the best examples and learn why they are the best examples, and then apply not necessarily just the forms and details, but the design principles that gave rise to the forms. We shouldn't limit ourselves to copying past buildings, but we shouldn't make the mistake of thinking we have nothing to learn from them. Maine's great Shingle-Style architect John Calvin Stevens knew that in 1889, when he and his coauthor, Albert Winslow Cobb, described this process in their book *Examples of American Domestic Architecture*. They said:

It is easy enough to build in a merely

original fashion; we have most abundant and most lamentable evidence of that. But the rational, virtuous types—the worthy models in Architecture, prepared for us by past experience and best fitted to our present needs, are few; and are positive, graceful, orderly in their nature. Holding faithfully to these tried and proven types as bases of our modern design, we may nevertheless find plentiful opportunity for variety in the work based upon them. Just as, by the ever-varying disposition of a few constant elements of ocean and lake and river, snow and verdure, plain, hill-slopes, crags and cloud-swept sky, God builds us a setting for our lives—a setting new to us every morning and fresh every

evening—infinitely changing, ever appealing to us in some new grouping as we go.

There is a lesson here for those of us who will be restlessly seeking to invent new vagaries, unseen before, wherewith to compose the little structures we are building beneath the eternal dome of heaven.

As well weary of the elm tree as of the chaste Ionic column. As well weary of the sky itself as of the sturdy Norman arch that so denotes support.

Left — *A low arch defines the space of an inglenook around the fireplace.* ***Above*** — *Curved, shingled supports appear to be straining under the weight of the roof.*

It often seems that we as a culture have lost the passion for building that Stevens and Cobb displayed. Certainly we are less likely to indulge in the kind of rhetoric they used. Our houses seem too often to be commodities, changeable and transitory. When we see the intense enthusiasm of James Beyor and Jane Goodrich, we should ask ourselves whether we love our houses as much, and if the honest answer is that we do not, we should ask what we can do to make our homes into something that will inspire in us the same kind of passion that Stevens and Cobb expressed.

Above — *Stenciled fir branches are an informal version of more geometric patterns common in the 19th-century. This kind of subtle updating prevents the house from being a dry replica.*

Part Four
BUILDING NEW HOUSES

Thus far we have looked at how people have made existing buildings—or, in the case of Kragsyde, a house that once existed—into homes that fit their needs. Let us turn now to situations where the land is all there is, and the task is to fit a new house into it. I hope that by having started from examples of existing houses and our responsibility to them, we can now see how the same careful attention to the existing landscape can make a new building seem to belong to its setting. Whether that landscape is a patch of untamed woods or an old farm pasture, designers who pay attention to the particulars of the site achieve a harmony that is too often not apparent in the repetitive suburbs that hold most new houses.

The examples that follow have no consistent architectural style. They do, I believe, share a kindred respect for the land. In the twentieth century, the idea that modern design should proceed only from the function that a particular house was to perform became a creed for many architects. Le Corbusier called the house a "machine for

Traditional elements in a thoroughly modern house in Deer Isle.

New house interiors can be light (below) or dark (right). **Opposite** *— What makes a house good is how it fits into the landscape.*

living," and designs that followed this manifesto did, indeed, come to resemble machines like factories and ships more than what we think of as houses. By the 1960s modern design came to be regarded by young architects as stuck in a formal rut. "Modern" had come to mean "flat-roofed box," even though earlier modern works had displayed great variety. Some of the period's architects, like Richard Meier, looked back to the early modern period of greater formal invention and chose as models Le Corbusier's early designs.

Others, like Edward Larrabee Barnes, who designed the Haystack School on Deer Isle, went more directly on the attack against the flat-roofed box and introduced such "innovations" as a sloping roof and exterior walls made not of glass and concrete, but of wooden boards or even shingles. These architects were afraid that their modernist predecessors would dismiss them as traditionalists who hated the whole modern movement, rather than respecting them as reformers who sought to restore flexibility, variety, and complexity, which they saw as being lost in the rigorous simplification practiced by the modernists. They avoided the accusation of traditionalism by making their shapes different from traditional buildings. They shunned symmetry, preferring shed roofs that sloped in one direction to gables that rose to a central peak before descending harmoniously back toward the ground.

They especially avoided traditional double-hung windows with small panes in favor of plain glass and casement windows. In this latter practice, they were following

the dictates of Frank Lloyd Wright, who had stigmatized double-hung windows by calling them "guillotines," and who had advocated the casement as a way of bringing the outside in by figuratively reaching out toward the landscape with the embracing arm of the outswinging window. It is also true that this architectural movement coincided with the social stresses of the Vietnam War and the youth "revolution," and the buildings of the period seem in retrospect to have a fragmented and disharmonious quality that reflects the lack of unity in society at the time.

Since then there has been a gradual reintroduction of more overtly traditional elements such as gable roofs and guillotine windows. In particular, architects and historians have discovered the virtues of the kind of house that preceded the ubiquitous Colonial Revival that swept America at the turn of the twentieth century. This was Vincent Scully's "Shingle Style," which we saw epitomized by Kragsyde (page 106). The rigors of functionalism have been softened by the integration of environmentalism, and a healthy flexibility has reemerged in the design of houses that are more than radical, polemical statements of principle.

This has not been the only shift in house design. Modern houses have become more complex without forsaking their allegiance to the principles of early-modern designs. Moreover, other styles such as log houses and even Colonial-inspired, white-clapboard traditional buildings have been used as models for contemporary house designs. There is no one orthodoxy anymore, and that has been a great advance.

Lang House, Tenants Harbor

John Silverio

We begin with an example of the new Shingle Style. As architects encountered the Maine landscape in the 1980s, they rediscovered the principles established in the 1880s. Henry Hobson Richardson had been followed by William Ralph Emerson, Peabody and Stearns, Stevens and Cobb, and a whole generation of like-minded designers whose first loyalty was to making buildings that fit the land and that used the architectural language of rural America—stone foundations and shingled walls and roofs.

That movement had evolved in two directions: one was the stricter Colonial Revival, which in turn was attacked by Modernists, who saw any copying of old forms as dishonest. Modern architecture, however, seemed to impose its own rigid orthodoxy, and architects soon tried to bring back some of the naturalism of the previous styles. At first they were shy about it and pretended to use traditional language ironically, "quoting" a building element but using it in ways that made clear

they weren't being traditional. This style was called "post-modernism," and the name showed that these designers were more concerned with attacking modernism than achieving an architecture that stood on its own.

The other direction the Shingle Style had taken was toward the Arts-and-Crafts bungalow, a simpler house design that was easily prefabricated and sold by mail order. These usually had hipped roofs so the walls could all be the same height, but like their Shingle-Style predecessors they tended to be modest in scale and built of native materials that would blend with their surroundings. As architects looked around for alternatives to modernism and post-modernism, they were attracted by the simplicity and "truth to nature" of the Shingle Style.

The type had many attractions. It was genuine, a way of building derived from the common experience of

Opposite — *The roofs descend and reach out, while angled wings and broad steps anchor the house to the ground.* **Left** — *The counterflow fireplace warms the center of the house while (below) a gently arched window echoes the shape of the fireplace and softens the opening to the view.*

builders over several decades. This style was historically respectable, but it was less burdened than Colonial or Victorian or Gothic, with their requirements for explicit historic correctness. Forms and elements could be combined as suggested by the plan or the landscape. Form still followed function, but not with the reductive simplification of machine-based modern buildings. It respected the environment by using natural materials and by using shapes that harmonized with the natural contours of the landscape. And, finally, it made possible buildings that felt like homes, not like museums or offices.

This house in Tenants Harbor is a good example of the style. Lincolnville architect John Silverio took the basic hipped bungalow and tied it to the land with angled extensions for the garage and porch. He brought light down into the typically dark bungalow interior by adding a windowed cupola on the roof. Terraces and porches low enough not to need railings extend the house into the landscape. Wide overhangs are kept from feeling heavy by the absence of trimmed edges. Simple, traditional windows and doors are relieved by the one gently arched window facing the best view, a subtle gesture in keeping with the modesty of the design. The interior continues the theme of simplicity and the Shingle-Style sense of flowing, continuous space.

Above and Opposite — *A porch with chairs leads to the open landscape. The progression asks us to be at home in the outdoors, while providing a retreat to shelter when needed.*

Top — *Sloping roofs are punctuated with dormers that bring in daylight in tiny glimpses or broad expanses.* **Above** — *A pyramidal garage is linked by an open walkway instead of a cramped mudroom.* **Opposite** — *Rough steps emphasize the relation of finished house and unfinished nature.*

Log House, Chebeague Island

Tim Bullock and Joe Waltman

If Silverio's bungalow conveys the simplicity of the summer cottage, this house on Chebeague Island evokes the mystery of Maine's dense northern woods. The owners had originally intended to build a shingle cottage, but visits to Colorado made them fall in love with houses built of real logs.

Log cabins began to be erected in New England, primarily by Swedish immigrants, long before Colorado was developed by arriving gold prospectors and settlers. Their

use as vacation houses grew from the sporting camps of the Maine and Adirondack woods. They became high fashion when the rich began to build the Great Camps of the Adirondacks. Such complexes as J. P. Morgan's Uncas set the style for camps constructed of logs much more massive than structurally necessary.

This house is an elegant example of its type. Its logs were cut and fit by Ontarians Tim Bullock and Eric Weibe, specialists in solving the problems of working

Opposite — *Dark logs and wood shingles evoke the Maine woods.*
This page — *Logs invite the builder to add other details made from small peeled sticks. Window and door heads have to allow for shrinkage.*

with two-foot-diameter white pine timbers. In 1991 they preassembled the frame in Canada before trucking it to Chebeague Island, where Joe Waltman's company had prepared the site. Waltman and his foreman, Bob Kemper, were responsible for finishing the interior, as well as adding the rails and balconies, and details like the branching supports for the mantel.

There is, of course, a question about the environmental impact of building a house out of more trees than necessary —even if they are Canadian. Certainly log houses began as a response to the overabundance of trees and the shortage of labor needed for trimming them square. Using that style today, when factory-milled lumber is abundant and "king's pines" are scarce, can make us uneasy. What goes a long way toward answering the ecological question is the beauty of the result and the celebration of wood as tree rather than two-by-four.

Many companies now make log homes. Most of those use logs that are highly "regularized," or sawn into uniform widths that fit together with little of the special craftsman-ship evident in the Chebeague house's lovingly finished

Above — *A roof terrace provides escape from the dark interior. Note the leaded glass windows, evocative of 17th-century houses.*
Opposite — *Of course, the center of the house is a great hall.*

timbers. And, with the availability of standard packages, like the precut Victorian houses of the last century, the new "log" houses tend to look perched on their sites instead of carefully fit into them. This island house, with its dark exterior and its long, low roofs, seems at home on its landscape. The deeply shadowed entrance porch is like a cave, and the small windows and eyebrow dormer add light while preserving the sense of protective enclosure. Living inside is like being in the shelter of the forest itself.

English geographer Jay Appleton has written that he believes we as humans are most comfortable when we can look out over our landscape while at the same time having a sense that we can withdraw into the woods for protection—a pattern he calls "prospect and refuge." He sees this as dating to our earliest days as a species, when we lived on the edges of the African veldt and retreated to treetops or forests to escape predators. However fanciful this anthropological hypothesis may be, the idea is suggestive. Grant Hildebrand has shown how this principle can be used to analyze the houses of Frank Lloyd Wright, from the early ones not far removed from the Shingle Style to the later Usonian bungalows and his more extreme geometric exercises.

In this house, with its giant protective logs surrounding its inhabitants like a fortress but opening out into porches overlooking the sea, we can clearly see the contrast between the warm, safe interior and the open outdoors. We are invited to love both—in their season. It is not the choice of materials alone that makes a house a home; it is the care with which the site is understood and the forms of the house adjusted to express the qualities of

the site. As builder Waltman, who was originally skeptical about the idea of the log structure, says of the completed house, "It works there, and that surprises people. The house really feels like it belongs. Give it ten years, and it will look like it's been there for centuries."

Left — The rustic exterior softens the presence of the house and integrates it with the trees and lawns. *Top* — The dining room feels more like a cave than a house. *Above* — forked trunks give an almost anthropomorphic feel to the posts.

Deer Isle House

Winton Scott

A different method of belonging to a site is demonstrated by this decidedly nontraditional house designed by Winton Scott. Though clad in shingles and having roofs with traditional pitches and wide overhangs, this structure owes more to the modern concrete houses of Richard Neutra in California in the late 1920s than to the Shingle-Style cottages of the 1890s. The house rises up on cylindrical columns that evoke the early modern style as much as they do the trees that surround the house,

and the bold, cantilevered balconies are reminiscent of Fallingwater—a design by that ex-Shingle-Style architect Frank Lloyd Wright.

Yet the house does belong to its place and time. Since it was to be built in a dense stand of mature spruce, the owner hired a professional forester, D. Gordon Mott, to advise him on how to keep the trees around the clearing from being endangered. Mott said that cutting a hole in a forest makes the trees around it vulnerable to

Opposite — *The house is raised up to fill the hole in the tree canopy.* ***Above*** — *A tall central space is overlooked by interior windows and balconies, giving the feeling of a clearing surrounding by towers.*

Opposite — *The fireplace sits in an updated version of a Shingle-Style inglenook.* **Below left** — *Round posts and an exaggerated chimney respond to the tall trees surrounding the house.* **Below right** — *Vertical spaces and bridges enhance the treehouse feel of the interior.*

wind and that the house should be tall enough to replace the wind-resistant mass of the missing trees. Setting the house up on posts would also minimize the damage to the root mass of the remaining trees. Maine sporting camps were usually set on cedar posts and rocks rather than sunk in the freezing ground. So a design that may appear to be a stylistic anomaly for a Maine cottage actually results from conditions that respect and protect the forest.

Another way site impact was minimized was to use post-and-beam framing and insulated panels, which were preassembled, trucked to the site, and placed with a crane. As a result, the time the builders had to spend on foot at the site was reduced.

Finally, of course, the coastal site was not cleared. Maine law severely limits the amount of clearing of trees along the shorelines of lakes, ponds, rivers, and the sea. The restrictions were passed in reaction to the adverse environmental impact stemming from the increased runoff of soil and lawn fertilizers into the water, and the visual impact of the loss of the forest that formerly bordered the water. This design captures the spirit of the law as well as the letter. Rather than maximizing the amount of clearing and trimming allowed by the state, it leaves

the adjacent forest as untouched as possible. To see the water, you walk down a path to the shore, where the vista opens up as it did before the house was built.

If the Deer Isle house, even with its unusual forms, is appropriately reticent on the outside, the interior is a contrasting landscape of dramatic spaces. Like its modern predecessors, it consists of areas that open to each other both vertically and horizontally. Mrs. Van Rensselaer noted the diagonal vistas of Richardson's houses but she did not comment on vertical spaces, since they were usually limited to the stair hall. Here, the central space brings indoors the feeling of being on the forest floor, with the branching trees creating a canopy. Balconies and bridges draw the eye upward, and high windows let in light the way the forest canopy allows glimpses of sky. The fireplace inglenook, with its gabled "roof"—itself a classic Shingle-Style eliment—looks like a cabin in the forest, while the study, with its windows overlooking the "clearing" that is the sitting room, is like a tree house or a hunter's blind perched in the branches.

Architect Scott says the chief inspiration for the house was the owner's enthusiasm for the 1908 Gamble House of the Greene brothers in Pasadena, California. While it is possible to see the connection in elements like

the inglenook and the balconies and the overhangs of the roofs, it is clear that the inspiration of the Arts-and-Crafts masters has been filtered through an architectural sensitivity that draws as much or more on the masters of the modern movement. It is often assumed that to be appropriate for Maine a house must be designed in a style drawn from Maine's history. The Deer Isle house shows us that this is not always true. It may appear to be easier to use a traditional language—although designing well in a traditional style is like being able to speak a foreign language well—but the problem of fitting a house to its environment remains the same, whatever the style. Scott says the owner wanted a house that appeared "to have just happened, and not to have been overly influenced by any style of Maine architecture." Scott has, indeed, succeeded in the difficult assignment of making the building look as if it "just happened," but by means of his skill in drawing inspiration from widely disparate sources of inspiration.

Above — *A study perches above the interior clearing like a hunter's blind.* *Left* — *The hanging balcony evokes early modern houses like those of Wright or Schindler, but the overall effect of the house is that of a traditional cottage.*

Phippsburg House

Jeremiah Eck

At first glance, this 1995 house looks as if it is crying out for attention, the very thing I have repeatedly stressed should be avoided. Its owners, however, rejected a Shingle-Style design that strung out the waterside wall of the house in one long plane. They felt that this configuration made too much of an impact as seen from the water and that its long wall of windows could be the source of annoying reflections to boat operators. For them, this design worked better by breaking up the mass of the house into many angled fragments that blended it more effectively into the landscape. The strategy could be compared to that used in "stealth" aircraft, whose radar image is reduced by angling the plane's surfaces to deflect radio waves. Our first impression of busyness may be a case where the photographic process, by flattening out the spatial reality of a building into a two-dimensional perspective, does the house more of a disservice than usual. Brian Vanden Brink's images are among the best, but no photograph can really convey the experience of a house as a three-dimensional object.

The view from the waterside tells the story of the design. The building is broken into a cluster of separate, tiny houses, each with a separate function and each with its own traditional gable roof. These "houselets" are then clustered like fishing shacks around a harbor in an apparently random relationship. Rather than submitting to the overall discipline of a single idea, each appears to be following its own notion about where to turn. When, moving closer, we realize that the gable ends are not flat planes but are, themselves, angled to face yet different directions from the overall run of the gable roof, the spatial composition becomes complex to the point of being unsettling.

Yet from inside, these complexities resolve into indi-vidual spaces whose orientation to the outside makes sense. The screened porch is open on three sides and shaded by the overhang of the bedroom above. The living room is nearly a ceremonial apse, oriented toward the sacred axis of the sea and backlit from above by skylights to reduce the glare that a sea view generates. Hence, the interior winds around in a landscape of its own that mirrors the complexity of the rocky shore.

How is this kind of design arrived at? We have already talked about the owners' desire to keep the house from looking monolithic, but another practical necessity stemmed from the fact that this house replaced an existing, dilapidated cottage. Under Maine's strict regulations, a house that, like this one, is located within the state-mandated shoreland setback zone, can be rebuilt (or replaced) on its existing "footprint." However, no more

Opposite — *The varied elements were intended to make the house look smaller from the water, in the same way stealth airplanes deflect radar signals.* **Below** — *The other determining criteria were the views from the various rooms.*

Left — Interior details are high-tech modern, lit from unexpected angles. Below — The modern vocabulary is softened by a rough stone hearth. Opposite — The cluster of small elements looks more like a fishing village than a house. The rocky landscape is essentially untouched.

than 30 percent may be added to its volume or footprint, and none of that addition can be closer to the water's edge than the original house. As you can see from the complexity of even stating the regulations, the challenge of meeting them can be quite daunting. The architect has to first identify the physical footprint and calculate the existing volume of the original structure, and then design a plan that stays within the "envelope" defined by the regulations.

This process is really just a special case of the usual design process, which involves identifying the legal constraints on a site before work on the plans can begin. It is just more restrictive. All buildings are in effect monuments to the building codes that govern their construction, as much as they are to the desires of their owners and to the skills of their architect and builder. In this case, Boston architect Jeremiah Eck says, "We really played with the configuration to make it fit. We ended up twisting

Above — *Most windows look out to sea, but the kitchen eyes at the cliff while skylights bring in the sun.* **Below** — *Corner windows extend the panoramic view.* **Opposite** — *Wraparound glass and skylights above make the landscape part of the room.*

and turning and, finally, shoehorning it into the site." The aim was not, however, to play with forms for forms' sake, but to give each space its own view and its own character. The result was a success with the owners, who say, "What Jeremiah has created in this house is an amazing flow of space, enhanced by the light and the play of light. Because of all the angles, because of all the points at which light enters, it's a constant series of changes and surprises."

Hillside House, Yarmouth

Scott Simons

If Eck seems to have pushed the limits of complexity, the house that architect Scott Simon built for himself in 1999 in Yarmouth shows how modern elements can be integrated into a design that at first glance can seem extremely traditional. On the entrance side, the house looks more like a collection of barns without a house to go with them. It has plain trim and an overall shingle skin, but the sharply angled roof is more akin to the vernacular architecture of the Howe Hill farmhouse (page 54) than to

the more picturesque Shingle Style. The way the roofs descend in apparently random stages from the principal peak does tie the house down to the land, but the long entry porch is more the suggestion of a farmhouse "piazza" than a cottage "veranda." The treatment of the garage door—making it look like a sliding barn door—adds to the message that we are at a farm, not a cottage. The interior, however, gives the game away and sets up the surprise at the back. Detailing is strictly High Modern,

with flat surfaces and nontraditional hardware. The space inside what had appeared from the front to be a traditional entry hall immediately explodes vertically into what had seemed from the outside to be a simple shed. Inside, however, it is revealed as the principal great room. This space opens to the private rear yard via a wall of glass, punctuated by a chimney of block and concrete and slip-form stonework, not of traditional stone or brick. The expectations of vernacular convention are stripped away.

Seen from the backyard, the effect is jarring. It's as if the wall of the room was removed, like the side of a doll-house, so that all the activities inside are on display. The aggressive projection of the shed roof, supported by

Opposite — From the street the house looks like a conventional barn with a piazza attached. **Above** *— Inside, however, the architecture is emphatically modern.* **Below** *— The wall to the rear is almost all glass.* **Following Pages** *— While the basic barn shape is closed, the living room looks like an open porch.*

massive timbers, allows no softening of the effect. What does, ultimately, return the house to its environmental context is the bracketing of this big glass shed by the solid mass of the house to the right, now revealed as a stack of bedrooms rather than a barn, and by the shingled wall and dormer roof to the left. The naked modernism of the structure is shielded from the neighbors and only indulged in the privacy of the rear yard. The great 16th-century English architect Inigo Jones said that a building should behave as a gentleman, conveying "graviti in publick places yet inwardly hath his imaginacy set on fire, sumtimes licenciously flying out." Simon's allegiance is to the excitement of modernism, but with an awareness of the decorum required for living in Maine.

Top — *Beams with exaggerated diagonal bracing frame the rough masonry chimney.* ***Above*** — *By contrast, the entry porch, looks almost rustic.* ***Right*** — *Stairs from the great room wind up behind shelves to the bedrooms above.*

Rosenzweig House, Blue Hill

Elliot and Elliot

Aprime example of how far modern architects have come toward the reintegraton of traditional forms is this complex of house, studio, and barn. If at first glance the buildings appear to be historic structures that have had a little upgrading, a more careful study reveals that they are very precise expressions of careful modernist space planning, drawing materials and details from the language of Maine vernacular. In this Blue Hill house from 1997, architects Elliot and Elliot have successfully combined the two modes of usually distinct approaches into a singular unity.

One way you can tell that this is not an ordinary farm complex is the wall that defines the lawn. The low stone wall and the related terraces were installed by Freshwater Stone and Brickwork's Jeff Gammelin, a master of careful stone craft. These are not rough barriers between pastures but a clear geometric ordering of the space on which the buildings sit. The nearest analogy to

the court and its buildings might be the Ryoanji stone garden in Kyoto, whose carefully placed boulders sit in a gravel "sea" contained by the walls of the courtyard. Something of the same formal repose is evident in the siting of the three buildings of the Ronsenzweig house within its rectangular court.

The buildings themselves are more like those of the Shaker communities, especially the one in Maine at Sabbathday Lake (page 13). The owners, their builder, and the architects agreed that Shaker simplicity should guide the design, and Thoreau's principle "Simplify, simplify!" became a rallying cry. Using standard materials and windows that deviate from tradition only by being larger and more vertically proportioned, the three buildings have a clarity and precision which invoke the spiritual intensity of Shaker design: "Hands to work and hearts to God." Even the narrow porch roof that runs the full length of two sides of the house seems to recall more the entry porch of a meetinghouse than a farmhouse porch meant

Opposite — *Three disciplined buildings sit in precise relationships in a stone-fenced meadow.* **Top** — *Inside, the elements are similarly related.* **Above** — *Traditional windows are oversized to admit more of the view.*

Above — *The Shaker-like buildings are carefully set at right angles and linked by stone paths.* **Opposite above and below left**— *The severity of the form is relieved by a porch supported by brackets like those on a train station.* **Opposite, below right**— *The studio brings in light through a variety of windows.*

Above — In the bedroom a chromed smoke pipe from the fireplace below interrupts but reflects the view. **Opposite** — *The regularly spaced windows and doors are more reminiscent of Grange halls than farmhouses, and thus add associations with public buildings to the already formal composition.*

for summer-kitchen chores. The windows are not varied to capture specific views; instead, they maintain the rigorous discipline of the whole complex, growing larger only where the gable end allows more space for the view toward the sea.

The interiors are just as disciplined, though hardly austere. The fireplace is a granite cube, and instead of running into a masonry chimney it vents through a steel pipe that passes in front of that large window upstairs. Though the fittings and appliances are of the best quality, their careful placement in these clean surroundings makes them seem less extravagant than they might appear in less well considered spaces.

The house and its outbuildings succeed in conveying the feeling of natural serenity that was the aim of the Shakers and the Zen monks. In this design, fitting in with nature does not mean imitating natural forms or camouflaging the house with natural materials and nearby trees and shrubbery. It means carefully demarking a zone in which human structures stand in a relationship of mutual respect to the natural environment. Like the Zen garden, the stone enclosure is a sanctuary in the wilderness, a place set apart—but not separate—from its neighbors.

Harrison House, North Bridgton

Stephen Blatt

The ideal picture of the Maine cottage that most of us, visitors and residents alike, carry in our heads probably sits by the water, nestled into the woods. One house that comes close to that ideal is the one Stephen Blatt designed in 1993 for Lynn Harrison on a point of land projecting into Long Lake in North Bridgton. The elements are all there: the lake and woods for a setting, a wide porch opening out from the house toward the lake, a steep gable roof punctuated with dormers, and wood-shingle walls.

This house replaces a log camp that was struck by lightning and that burned to the ground—less than a year after Harrison had bought it. More than thirty tall white pines surrounding the house were also destroyed. Harrison decided to rebuild. The house had to fit the restrictive zoning envelope we have explained before, and it had to be a worthy successor to the structure that had burned.

Solving the problem of providing space for year-round

Opposite — *Nothing symbolizes Maine more than the cottage by the lake. In this case the surrounding trees had burned, but new ones are already growing.* **Above** — *An open section of the porch roof lets light into the interior without breaking the line of the porch.*

Above — *At dusk the lights shimmer over the lake as the house disappears into its setting.* **Opposite** — *An unusual chimney of small flat stones anchors the center of the open interior.*

living within the restricted area allowed by the zoning, while at the same time respecting the forms and images of traditional camps, proved to be a challenge. The design, says Blatt, went through a dozen revisions before the final plans were settled on. Harrison's unwillingness to settle for less than what she considered to be the best solution was matched by Blatt's willingness to meet his client's needs. As with most of the houses we have seen, both new and renovated, the first floor is largely open but is divided into separate areas by changes in floor level and by the central chimney mass. Naturally finished wainscot contrasts with light plaster walls to keep the interior bright without losing the warmth of wood. Upstairs, bedrooms are tucked into spaces with steep ceilings. Ceilings flow into walls, and storage cubbyholes happen in the areas too short to stand in. Windows are

limited by the roof areas, and the dormers are not allowed to dominate the roof shape, even at the cost of limiting the available floor area.

The result, far from looking like a labored exercise, is a house that seems to belong where it is. It does not stick out nor call attention to itself. Harrison says, "It looks like an old cottage with all the classic lines, and it looks like it's been here for years—which was our primary goal from the beginning."

Right — The curve of the clawfoot tub is echoed in the curve of the window. *Below* — A high, naturally finished wainscot adds warmth, while light upper walls and ceilings brighten the interiors. *Opposite* — A "cottage window" of small panes above large ones is flanked by lower sash to fill a gable using traditional window elements.

Above — _At home in Maine._

EPILOGUE

In the previous pages, we have seen only a small sample of the wide variety of ways in which dedicated people have responded to the challenges of being at home in Maine. Not all of us are fortunate enough to be able to afford the kinds of houses—or indeed the kinds of house sites—that are shown in this collection. Even fewer are able or willing to go to the trouble of making their homes into places that truly meet their needs. Most of us take our houses as we find them and have enough to do maintaining them.

This book is not meant to leave us envying the lucky owners of these houses while we struggle with furnace repairs and the next coat of paint. My hope is that by looking at these examples of excellence, we can look at our own homes with new eyes and see opportunities to "brighten the corner where we are," as the old Salvation Army hymn says. What we should learn from studying houses like these is how the owners and their architects paid attention to the way in which the houses interact with their cultural and natural landscape. Everything we do has an impact on our surroundings, whether we live on an ideally located piece of shorefront or in the middle of a village or even in a subdivision of houses like our own. That impact can be negative or positive. We can embarrass our neighbors—and ourselves—or we can be respectful citizens, participating in a civic dialogue that raises community standards of excellence and goodwill.

Our homes, finally, can express our desires, but—in Mrs. Van Rensselaer's excellent phrase—"with a reticence that does not put the humblest village neighbor out of countenance." Too much of what we see praised seems to do the opposite, to flaunt our successes in our neighbors' faces. If there is anywhere in America where this should not be our goal, it is the state of Maine.

Brian Vanden Brink
Photographer
PO Box 419
Rockport, Maine 04856
Tel. 207-236-4035
brian@brianvandenbrink.com

Poore Houe, Standish
18th Century Reproductions
Rick Poore
230 Bonny Eagle Road
Standish, ME 04084
Tel. 207-642-4324

Donham House, Head Tide
Donham & Sweeney, Architects
Brett Donham
68 Harrison Avenue
Boston, MA 02111
Tel. 617-423-1400

Howe Hill Farm, Camden
Scholz & Barclay Architecture
John Scholz & Meg Barclay
PO Box 1057
Camden, ME 04843
Tel. 207-236-0777

Smithwick House, Boothbay Harbor
Coastal Designers &
Consultants Inc.
Martin Moore, Designer
PO Box 390
Southport, ME 04576
Tel. 207-633-2600

Boothbay Homebuilders
PO Box 142
Boothbay, ME 04537
Tel. 207-633-3818

Covington Design Assoc., Inc.
Cornelia Covington Smithwick,
ASID
3562 St. Johns Avenue
Jacksonville, Florida 32205
Tel. 904-384-8066

Lakeside Camp, Western Maine
Stephen Blatt Architects
10 Danforth Street
PO Box 583 DTS
Portland, ME 04112
Tel. 207-761-5911

Anderson House, Camden
Chris Glass, Architect
38 Chestnut Street
Camden, ME 04843
Tel. 207-236-8215
chris.glass@verizon.net

Thorn House, Bass Harbor
Christian Fasoldt, Architect
40 Pascal Avenue
Rockport, ME 04856
Tel. 207-236-6569

Susan Thorn, ASID
Susan Thorn Interiors, Inc.
88 N. Salem Road
Box 187
Cross River, NY 10518
Tel. 914-763-5265

**Maine Historic Preservation
Commission**
State House Station 65
Augusta, ME 04333
Tel. 207-287-2132

**Coaling Station, Little Diamond
Island**
Whitten & Winkelman Architects
Rob Whitten
37 Silver Street
PO Box 404 DTS
Portland, ME 04112
Tel. 207-774-0111

Lang House, Tennants Harbor
John Silverio, Architect
105 Proctor Road
Lincolnville, ME 04849
Tel. 207-763-3885

Cindy Lang Interior Design
PO Box 282
Tenants Harbor, ME 04860
Tel. 207-372-8906

Log House, Chebeague Island
Bullock & Company
Log Home Builders
Tim Bullock
PO Box 44
New Lowell, Ontario
Canada L0M1N0
Tel. 705-424-5222

Joe Waltman
Anastos & Nadeau
121 Main Street
Yarmouth, ME 04096
Tel. 207-846-0410

Deer Isle House
Winton Scott, Architect
5 Milk Street
Portland, ME 04101
Tel. 207-774-4811

Phippsburg House
Jeremiah Eck Architect, Inc.
560 Harrison Avenue
Suite 403
Boston, MA 02118
Tel. 617-367-9696

Hillside House, Yarmouth
Scott Simons Architects
Scott Simons
75 York Street
Portland, ME 04101
Tel. 207-772-4656

Rosenzweig House, Blue Hil
Elliott Elliott Norelius
Architecture
86 Main Street
PO Box 318
Blue Hill, ME 04614
Tel. 207-374-2566

Harrison House, North Bridgton
Stephen Blatt Architects
10 Danforth Street
PO Box 583 DTS
Portland, ME 04112
Tel. 207-761-5911